CW01512530

The Night They Went to Town

By

C G Fewtrell

ISBN: 978-1-916732-48-3

Published By: -

i2i
PUBLISHING

i2i Publishing.   Manchester.
www.i2ipublishing.co.uk

Introduction 1 (Reader, you can skip this bit if you like. I won't mind.)

Parents sometimes do terrible things.

Sometimes they do them for the right reasons.

That doesn't make anyone feel any better.

Dreadful things happen to us all, one time or another.

How should we cope?

Sometimes we take those dreadful things, put them in a steel box and wrap the box in chains and padlocks. Then we put the box in the boot of our imaginary car and drive down into the deepest, darkest corner of our memory and park it there, sometimes forever.

Sometimes something sneaks down there and opens up the boot.

"Look in here," it says, but usually we look away.

Another way of coping is to keep that memory always close at hand. To never let it rest, to let it shape our lives, as if nothing else important ever happened.

Though 99% of the rest of our lives could be more or less perfect, we allow that 1% to cloud it over, to flavour it with pain, to rain misery on ourselves and the people around us.

Like with most things, the best answer is usually found somewhere around the middle.

Maybe, if those memories resurface now and then of their own accord, find someone you can trust - someone like Gerry (you'll meet him in a minute) - and talk them out.

Introduction 2

Mommapig, the parent in this story, struggled with her memories, and who can blame her?

I'll be honest with you (always) – I like bacon.

I became a vegetarian once, and it was bacon that dragged me back into the world of carnivores.

But I would never – ever – eat a suckling pig.

I don't want to upset anyone who doesn't know, but a suckling pig is a piglet taken from its Momma after a very few weeks on this wonderful planet and eaten by humans.

Why?

I'm not going to preach or tell anyone that what I believe is better than what they believe but come on!

Maybe if I was starving to death, or my children were, maybe then I'd cook a baby piglet and maybe share it with my kids – depends how hungry I was and how big the piglet was – but just for pleasure? Because it's tender and sweet? No way.

Mommapig had suffered this unimaginable horror a couple of times over the years. She had produced several litters of beautiful piglets, only to see some of them removed before her milk ran out and never returned.

She was unutterably sad every time, but she had other piglets to raise so she got on with it, like all good mothers do.

Occasionally, something would spark a memory, and she would have to relate the whole story to whoever happened to be nearby.

Once she started, she couldn't stop, until every detail of her tragedy had been laid out and the tears were running down her cheeks.

She was talking it out, and each time she did so, the pain seemed a little less sharp, the memory a little less potent.

However, these things still shaped her life and sometimes affected her decision-making skills.

As, of course, they would…

Chapter 1

Momma Pig warning Leanne

Mommapig saw Wolves everywhere she looked:

In the closet.

Under the bed.

Round every corner.

Out the door.

Behind the door.

Behind the trees.

Behind the smiling faces of passing strangers.

So, when fashion among the young female farm animals extended to wearing a dab of gravy behind each ear, she decided things had gone far enough.

"No," she said. "No way. Are you mad?"

Leanne piglet looked at Mommapig like *she* was the one missing most of her brain.

"Shush, Momma," she said. "You're embarrassing me," for her friends were waiting at the door.

"Embarrassed?" Mommapig said. "I'd rather see you embarrassed than basted. Get that gravy washed off immediately, or you're going nowhere."

"It's not gravy," Leanne pointed out patiently. "It's perfume. Eau de Boeuf, and everyone's wearing it."

"I'm not wearing it," Mommapig said. "I wouldn't be seen dead wearing it."

"Yes, you would," Grandmommapig joined in. "That's exactly when you *would* be seen wearing it, with a nice pair of roast potato earrings."

As usual, everyone ignored her.

"But Momma," Leannepig said, "I don't see what the problem is."

"Exactly," Mommapig said. "You don't see problems anywhere. That's why you have a mother to point them out to you."

Momma's problem was this: she wanted all her piglets to be safe, she wanted to warn them about all the dangers the world had waiting for them:

The holes in the ground they might fall into and never arise from.

The trucks on the main road that could squish them in the blink of a snake's eye.

The snakes that could slither out of the bushes and swallow them whole, leaving not a trace until they spat out the bones a couple of weeks later.

The humans in town with their knives and forks and greedy slobbering lips.

Most of all, she wanted to warn them about the Wolves. The sly, sneaky, perpetually hungry Wolves, with their cold, cold eyes and their sharp, sharp teeth.

But how could she warn and protect and arm her

children against all these terrors, without leaving them too terrified to ever leave her side?

It wasn't easy, and sometimes she thought maybe she was going over the top, but what could you do when youngsters were going around, almost *inviting* the Wolves home to dinner?

Grandmommapig didn't worry about going over the top. She just said the first thing that came into her head and never showed any regret.

Listen…

"I wish your father was here," Mommapig told Leanne.

"He *is* here," Grandmommapig said. "Most of him, anyway," and she nodded her head in the direction of the shed where Farmer Morris kept his freezers. Mommapig was not impressed.

"Mother!" she snapped. "Shut up and keep your snout out."

Fortunately, the younger pigs never listened to anyone older than their mother, and barely even listened to her.

There was a knock on the door; Leanne's friends were becoming impatient.

"Come in," Mommapig called to them, anxious to see the latest ludicrous fashion trends.

First in was Turkey Tess, wearing a very attractive cranberry necklace, all glistening and shining round her delicately wrinkled throat.

"Hi."

Next came Lulu Lamb, trotting in with a lovely frilly paper sock clinging to each of her lovely frilly ankles.

Carolyne Calf followed, with all the best cuts of meat beautifully outlined on her body with lipstick.

Mommapig's eyes rolled up in despair.

Grandmommapig tossed Leanne an apple.

"Here," she said. "Pop that in your mouth…you may as well go the whole hog."

For once, Mommapig agreed with Grandmommapig.

Chapter 2

When she was younger, Mommapig remembered having the same arguments, wanting to go out with her friends to play in the woods, and hating her mother (Grandmommapig) for making her stay where she could see her. And in those days, nobody was going out dressed for dinner or trotting round like a walking menu, and she was certain there weren't half as many Wolves around as there seemed to be now.

In those days, you knew where you were with Wolves - usually running like mad from their slobbering jaws, or, if you were unlucky, disappearing between them – but now? Now the Wolves were sneaky and came in all shapes and sizes. She thought about her very own cousin, Uncle Buzz...

Uncle Buzz was called uncle by everyone, because everybody loved him. Anything for anyone he'd do, sometimes even without being bribed. Then, one day, he'd come across a pile of old apples, fermenting in the sun. Without stopping to think, he stuffed in his snout and chomped his way through the lot, only to find he could no longer walk in a straight line, his vision was blurred, and he had the worst attack of hiccups this side of Kazakhstan.

That wasn't the worst of it though.

That evening, while everyone was sitting outside, chatting and watching piglets playing in the sun, a familiar figure appeared on the edge of town, walking unsteadily, occasionally drifting towards a ditch by the side of the road before regaining momentum and direction and heading straight towards the community trough.

At first Mommapig, or Shirleypig as she was then known, didn't recognize Uncle Buzz, but when she did, she thought he must be ill, and approached him to see if she could help. The closer she got to him, the more uncomfortable she became. His eyes were red and bore an expression she had never seen before

He looked at her, but not *at* her.

More like *through* her, like he not only didn't recognize her, but couldn't even *see* her. Shirleypig turned her head and followed his gaze: if it was focused at all, it was focused on the younger piglets behind her, and if pigs have lips, he was licking his.

Shirleypig stood in front of him.

"Buzz," she said. "Uncle Buzz?"

He blinked a couple of times, seemed to be calling his mind back from a million light years away, and eventually settled on Shirleypig's face. There was a microsecond when she thought he knew who she was, then a chill as she stared into his eyes and realized Buzz no longer lived inside this head. Those eyes, red and watery, belonged to no pig she had ever met, no pig *anyone* had ever met, for these were the pitiless eyes of a killer.

The eyes of a hungry hunter.

The eyes of a Wolf.

And no one was safe.

Fortunately, Buzz was shepherded away by some of the elder pigs who'd seen this phenomenon before and knew how to deal with it before anyone got hurt.

But Uncle Buzz was never the same again. For a start, no one ever trusted him from that day forward, knowing what lurked inside him, and his life became intolerable. until Farmer Morris invited him to take a drive to see a friend of his who ran a therapeutic abattoir in a nearby village.

Chapter 3

Meanwhile, back in the present, Leanne was sulking.

"I want to go out with my friends," she said. "Why can't I?"

"You can," Momma told her. "So long as you stay where I can see you."

"What's the point of that? I may as well stay in the house with Grandmomma."

"That works for me," Momma said.

"Me too," said Grandmomma. "She can scrape the crusty skin off my trotters, they been playin' up something rotten."

"Momma, *please*," Leanne begged. "I promise I'll be good."

Momma looked at her daughter, torn between the love and the fear every parent suffers. Leanne sensed her weakening.

"I'll be careful Momma," she said. "And I won't wear Eau de boeuf or anything like that. Please."

"Who else is going?" Momma wanted to know.

"There's loads of us," Leanne said. "And Gerry Bull's going to be there," she added, knowing Mommapig thought the world of him, because he was big and strong, and also polite and very sensible.

"Ha!" Grandmommapig splurted. "I knew his dad

– Terry Bull," she said. "And he certainly lived up to his name, I can tell you."

Mommapig ignored her.

"And where are you thinking of going?" she asked Leanne.

"Just into town," Leanne answered all nonchalant, like the way she said it might not make Mommapig blow her stack.

"WHAT?" Mommapig squealed, blowing her stack.

"WHAT?" Grandmommapig joined in and accidentally spat her false teeth into the fireplace.

"WHAT?" shouted Lulu Lamb, almost frightened out of her tiny mind by all the sudden noise. "Who's seen a Wolf?"

"WHAT?"

Now everyone was screaming, running round in a panic and trying to hide from the non-existent Wolf.

Apart from Grandmommapig. She was snuffling around in the fireplace, trying to find her teeth and getting covered in soot. When she found them, she popped them in and turned round triumphantly, black as an Irish coal-merchant.

"Gotcha!" she crowed, baring her gleaming gnashers, and everybody screamed again, thinking she was a Wolf who'd dropped down the chimney from an entirely different story.

Eventually everyone calmed down, and Mommapig gave Leanne her orders.

"You can go out," she said, "but definitely not to town." Leanne looked at the floor. "And I don't want you leaving the village and I want you to stay near Gerry at all times." Leanne sighed. "And I want you in the house at half-past nine, okay?"

Leanne looked at the ceiling.

"Okay," she said. "Can I go?"

"Promise you won't go to town."

"Didn't I just say okay?"

"And you won't leave the village."

"MOMMA! Is that how little you think of me?"

Momma gave up and waved Leanne and her friends out the door.

Outside, they met up with a few other friends. At once, Vinnie the Veal opened his mouth. "Come on, we have to get to town. Where've you all been?"

Lululamb and TurkeyTess stood still and scoured their tiny brains for the answer, but now they came to think about it, they weren't quite sure.

"Er…I think we…" said Lulu

"Didn't we…" Tess began, then trailed off, pointing her beak one way and then another, as though deep in thought, even though she had already forgotten what it was she was trying to think about. Leanne trotted forward.

"Come on then," she said. "Let's go."

Carolyne, who wasn't quite as stupid as Tess and Lulu, spoke up.

"Er, didn't your mum say you couldn't go to town?"

Leanne smiled at her.

"She said a few things if I recall," she said. "I know she said be back by half-past nine, and she said I had to stay near Gerry. I don't think she expects me to remember every single little thing she says, really. Do you?"

Before Carolyne could answer, Leanne turned to Gerry, who had just arrived.

"Where are you going, Gerry?" She smiled her sweetest smile, right in his face.

"Um, I thoughts we were going to town," he said, looking round at everyone else for confirmation.

"Well, that settles it," Leanne said. "My mum said I have to stay right next to you all evening, and if you're going to town, I better go to town as well," and she looked at Carolyne, pointed her nose in the air and closed her eyes, as if to say, 'find the holes in that argument, if you think you're so smart' and she trotted off beside Gerry as though she didn't have a care in the world.

Silly pig.

Chapter 4

They set off without a care in the world. It was only a one mile walk into town and the weather was warm and pleasant.

Normally, animals going to town travelled in farmer Morris's truck, and it was usually a one-way trip. No one ever discussed this fact, and most of the time effortlessly managed to not even think about it.

What was the point? Thinking or talking about it wasn't going to change it, and if you didn't think or talk about it, there was always the chance that it would never even happen.

If the subject ever came up - for instance if one of the younger animals noticed someone was missing - the answer would be, "Oh, they've gone to the retirement farm." Or: "They've gone to the seaside." By the time it became obvious that no one was coming *back* from the seaside or retirement farm, most of the animals, having mercifully short memories, had forgotten all about them.

Leanne strolled at the back with Gerry Bull, not only because Mommapig had insisted, but also because she liked Gerry, and she always felt safe when he was around.

Not that she didn't feel safe anyway. She thought Mommapig was overly cautious, to say the least, and what harm could befall anyone on such a lovely evening?

All around them, the green and yellow fields stretched lazily away, until the distant blue mountains rose up to meet the cloudless sky.

Just as the sun began to feel a smidgeon too warm, they arrived at the Lavender Woods and entered a perfect dappled shade, a gentle breeze nudging the branches above them and cooling their glowing faces. As well as Lavender, the woods were full of flowers, herbs and luscious grass, and the friends stopped often to bend down and nibble the free banquet. Better still, there were thick bushes heavy with raspberries, full of sweetness and the world seemed almost too generous and kind.

By the time they left the woods, the sun was halfway down the sky and the perfect afternoon was giving way to a perfect evening.

"Move to the side," Gerry called out, and all the young animals moved to allow a large vehicle to crawl past them. It was a truck pulling a huge trailer made of wood. There were two decks to the trailer, and there were gaps in the wood, like windows without glass, and behind each window was at least one face belonging to a sheep. There were about forty windows in all, meaning there were at least eighty sheep on board, and as the truck passed, the animals outside could smell and feel the warmth emanating from the animals within.

"Where are they going?" Lululamb asked as they watched the truck trundle away down the lane.

Vinnie the veal, also known as Vinegar Joe, started

to speak but Gerry nudged him aside, landing him in the ditch.

"Them's off to the seaside I expects," Gerry said. "Looks like a day trip to me."

"At this time of day?" Vinegar Joe said, climbing out of the ditch and not getting why Gerry had pushed him there in the first place. Gerry glared at him and pushed him back in.

"Them's probably on their ways *back* from the seaside then," Gerry said.

On they strolled without a care in the world. Town was now only half a mile away, and their path led though winding lanes where birds sang from the hedgerows and cute, furry animals peeped nervously at them from the overgrown roadside ditches.

They passed through two picturesque villages with their thatched cottages, ponds and greens, then they were on the final stretch, a long road with pavement on both sides, so they could walk safely, even though the traffic was a bit heavier. Not this evening though. This evening, with the sun painting the sky pink and purple as it began its long descent towards the horizon, the road was quiet. There was just the odd truck ambling its way home, and the occasional cart trundling along, loaded with golden hay, spilling parts of its precious cargo into the path of the friends, who stopped selflessly to clean up the street with their mouths.

Turkey Tess occupied herself by asking local

worms to join her for a snack, even though she barely knew them, then they were all on their way, excitement mounting as they neared the end of their journey.

To the animals, Town was the big city. The crowded, noisy streets, the traffic, the absence of grass, the overflowing shops and restaurants; everything was so different to their normal, day to day experience.

Lululamb was bouncing up and down, wanting to do everything at once. Carolyne Calf was in a daze – there was so much happening, her brain couldn't cope, and for a minute, she thought she was going to faint. Everyone else felt a little the same, but Gerry gathered them together and spoke.

"Right," he said. "Anybody wants to wander off, they can go now, they can, or laters, but we meets back here, by the trough, no laters than 9 o'clock. And I suggests we stays in pairs, at least. It may not seems like a dangerous place, what with the sun still shining and everywhere crowded an' everything, but trust me; things can turn nasty, very fast round here they can, so keeps to the main streets and don't goes off anywheres on your own."

Before you could say 'Abracadabra,' or even 'Shish kebab,' the friends had scattered.

And in the shadows between the stores, and in the doorways, and in all the little crannies where shifting pools of darkness gathered, eyes watched and shapes moved restlessly, lips were licked and teeth seemed to grow a little sharper.

Chapter 5

Leanne stayed with Gerry, because she had promised, and because she enjoyed staying with him. He didn't say a lot, but what he said was usually funny, or sensible, or both. Leanne was quite sensible herself, apart from going to town against Mommapig's wishes, and she had no intention of getting herself into trouble or danger of any description. She was there to enjoy the thrill of something new, and to be home on time without anyone being any the wiser.

And if Momma found out later, as doubtless she would, then Leanne would be able to say, "Well, I told you I'd be safe and there was nothing to worry about," and Momma would shake her head and say, "Well don't you ever do anything like that again," and the whole thing would be over and done with.

What she didn't know, was that come nine o'clock, when everyone was supposed to meet, she and Gerry would be next to the trough, but none of the others would be anywhere in sight.

The atmosphere in Town had somehow changed.

The lights were still bright, but the surrounding darkness seemed somehow darker. The strangers passing by seemed stranger, more alien, the traffic more threatening, the sounds more confusing and louder.

By five-past nine, Gerry was looking annoyed.

By ten past, he was looking worried.

"I better go and looks for 'em," he said, but he seemed reluctant, maybe because he feared the worst, or maybe because he didn't want to leave Leanne on her own.

Leanne was agitated too, and not just because all her friends were missing.

"I have to get home," she said. "If I don't leave now, it'll be even darker, and I'll also be late."

"I knows," Gerry said. "I'd much rather you was with me, but if you wants to set off, I'll try and catch you up. I don't thinks I'll be looking very long," he added. "Our friends has been really stupid…"

Leanne wanted to burst into tears but she put on a brave face and pointed it in the direction of home. "Please hurry up," she said to Gerry, and off she set.

She remembered the journey to town, and thought she would be safe enough, even if all the friends who'd accompanied her had now disappeared. It had been a pleasant journey, and she couldn't remember anything that might frighten or threaten her now, on the way back.

However, the sun had continued its gentle slide towards the horizon, and as the shadows lengthened all around, uneasiness slipped an arm around her shoulders.

"I'll walk fast," she told herself. "Then I'll be home quicker, and there should still be a little bit of light." She put on a bit of speed, then slowed down again. "If I go too fast," she thought, "Gerry won't be able to catch up, and I'll be all alone, all the way."

And so will Gerry, she thought, and felt afraid, more for him than for herself. She stopped and looked back towards the town. She'd only been walking a few minutes, but already town seemed quite far away, the streets less crowded, the sounds becoming muffled. Darkness had crept a little closer, and she thought about her friends and what might have happened to them, and she thought about Gerry and what might happen to him...

...and, also, what might happen to *her*.

"Oh please come now," she whispered, willing Gerry to appear at the edge of town, trotting towards her, but no one appeared, and she turned back to the road.

She felt her ears stiffen, then twitch, and realized she was listening hard to every tiny sound, checking in case she was being tracked or followed or stalked by some malevolent beast. The silence was almost painful, but then it was smashed as a car roared by, its headlights illuminating the road ahead. As the car disappeared in the distance, swallowed up by the encroaching night, the darkness seemed to take a few more steps towards her, and she shivered involuntarily.

"Get going," she said to herself. "Everything's fine."

She continued along the road, trying not to think

about what might have happened to all her friends. They had all been so happy, all the way there. Who would think anything could happen to them, in broad daylight as well.

It wasn't broad daylight now, though, and the first village she came to seemed to be deserted. Previously, it had seemed a very welcoming place, with its thatched cottages and pond and greens. Now there were no ducks or swans, or anybody else, and even the thatched cottages seemed to peer at her from under their fringes, frowning, as if to say, "*She'll* come to a sorry end…"

She carried on, glad to leave the village, but then hurrying so she could reach the next one. At least in the villages there were more lights and less places for Wolves to hide than out here in the open.

But when she got to the next village, it was worse. While the first village felt as though everyone had gone to bed early, this one felt utterly abandoned, as though everyone had simply decided to leave.

Or as if something had made them run away.

Something big.

And furry.

With sharp teeth and long claws…

"Stop it!" Leanne told herself. "Just get a move on and stop being a baby."

She tiptoed through the village, convinced something was watching her, feeling eyes on the back of her neck, imagining footsteps following, always following, but whenever she dared to glance behind, all she saw were shadows.

"Oh Momma," she whispered. "Why didn't I listen to you?"

On she went.

The lane twisted and turned, just as it had before, but Leanne couldn't remember anything sinister about those twists and turns as they'd made their way towards Town. Now, they seemed specifically designed to hide Monsters and Wolves, cunningly shaped so every time Leanne thought she was a little bit safer, she would turn one corner and find another one waiting for her, fifty yards further on.

And the ditches!

Earlier they had been colourful dips alongside the road, full of squirrels and mice and friendly little creatures who had been more frightened of Leanne than she could be of them. Now, though, the ditches looked like deep, dark pits, probably bottomless, or filled with dank and murky water. And the eyes that peered out now seemed larger, suspicious, malignant.

"Oh Gerry, where are you?" She looked back up the road but still all she saw were shadows, and now they seemed to be moving, or lurking in groups, discussing her, plotting their next move…

Something rustled in the ditch beside her, as though that something was moving through dry and brittle reeds, and then it stopped, and then it moved again, faster this time, and Leanne felt her heart leap, as though the thing was coming for her.

The noise grew ever more frantic, and was joined by another, as though something small was being pursued by something large, and then there was a final swishing and scrambling and scraping, then a pitiful squeal, and then nothing, just grass swaying gently in the breeze.

Leanne gave a shudder and marched onwards, quicker than before.

"I must be home soon," she thought. "Isn't this where the truck went past, taking the sheep to the seaside? Or bringing them back?" She couldn't remember. She wished *she* was at the seaside, or even better, back at home. She thought about Mommapig, and how she worried about her and tried to look after her, and this was her reward.

She thought about Grandmommapig, sitting in the corner, always grouchy and saying such crazy things, and she wished she were at home with her now, listening to her going on and on about the good old days, when the words 'suckling' and 'pig' formed a phrase that brought joy to Pigs' hearts, not fear and terror, and when the words 'factory' and 'farm' were never seen out together, holding hands in public like it was the most natural thing in the world.

Leanne wished she'd stayed home and scraped the dead skin off Grandmomma's trotters. Never again would she choose fun and adventure over scraping dead skin off ancient trotters, if only she could get home safe tonight.

"Look," she said to herself, noticing some flattened grass by the side of the path. "Isn't that where Vinegar Joe fell in the ditch?"

"No," another voice in her head came back. "It's where Gerry *pushed* him into the ditch."

Leanne laughed at the memory, but then another voice inside her said: "Are you sure? Are you sure that isn't where something just crawled *out* of the ditch? Something big and furry with big sharp – "

"Stop!" Leanne shouted at the voices in her head. "Whose side are you on anyway?"

She started to trudge on weary legs. The journey hadn't seemed this long earlier on, and certainly not as scary, but now the worst was to come, for she had forgotten all about the Lavender Woods.

In the evening, with the sun shining down, the woods had been a pleasant shelter, a charming and beautiful section of the journey. They had seemed so peaceful and harmless, why *should* she have remembered them, and dreaded returning the same way, several hours later?

With her head down, concentrating on moving fast and keeping the voices in her head quiet, Leanne had gone some way before she sensed a subtle change in her surroundings. Maybe it was the silence, or maybe there were a few more leaves upon the ground. Maybe the woods smelt different, or her eyes had sensed the last of the weakened sunlight being blotted out.

Whatever it was, when Leanne lifted her head, she was startled to find she was already deep within the woods, surrounded by trees and bushes. She almost panicked, and thought about retracing her steps, but it was further to go back than it was to go on, so she had no choice but to keep trudging forwards.

She had never been so frightened in her life, and peering ahead into the gloom of the forest, her legs began to shake, her bottom lip began to quiver, and tears started fighting one another for the privilege of being the first to trickle down her pretty cheeks.

"Keep going," she told herself. "It's not far now," but she could barely put one foot in front of another, so utterly terrified had she become.

"Cerr-ackk!"

Something was moving, off to the side, a fair distance away. Leanne froze, waiting to hear the sound again.

"Cerr-ackkk!"

There it was again. Was it closer? She couldn't tell. She stopped breathing. She listened...

For a minute, nothing.

Then…

"CerrrACKK!"

Definitely closer.

And louder.

What to do? She felt nailed to the floor, too petrified to move.

She'd heard about rabbits, who froze when confronted by a snake or something else in search of food, and she'd always laughed at them. "Who would stand there like a statue, when something wants to eat you up," she used to say. "What kind of fool would just wait to be captured, when they could simply run away and hide?"

Well now she was learning how it felt to be so frightened you couldn't move, even if moving meant you might save your own life.

"KER-RACCKKK!"

"Oh no!"

Whatever it was, was nearly upon her, and still she stood there, rooted to the earth just as securely as any of the trees that surrounded her. She tried her best to push forward, but now the friendly bushes, the ones with the luscious, delicious berries, were dragging her back, tearing at her skin with multitudes of tiny thorns, attempting to trip her with nasty, skinny branches, blocking her way and mocking her fear.

Something was crashing towards her through the same bushes and thorns, seemingly immune to the scratching and ripping and tripping, something so close, she imagined she could smell and feel the warmth of its existence, like the warmth of the sheep in the truck, a million years ago, but Leanne knew that whatever she was about to meet, it definitely wasn't sheep.

Leanne couldn't even imagine what kind of monster she was about to meet, or what it was about to do to her. All she could think about was Mommapig, and how sad she would be when they carried her bones back to the house.

And that is what saved her.

All the fear, all the dread, all the possibilities of what was about to happen, couldn't budge Leanne one inch either backwards or forwards or sideways.

But the thought of Mommapig's broken heart, visions of her tear-stained face and her endless nights of crying, gave Leanne an unexpected strength, and she found herself suddenly unglued and hurtling through the woods at record-breaking speed, the bushes receding behind her. The cracking and crashing continued, but whatever was chasing had no chance of catching her now, and she darted and dashed her way clear to the fields at the far side of the Lavender Woods.

Unfortunately, the worst was yet to come.

Chapter 6

Leanne stopped for a moment, catching her breath, and listening, carefully, to see if she were still pursued, but the sounds of her pursuers were distant now, and growing fainter, as though they had lost her trail, or picked up someone else's.

"Please don't let them find Gerry," she prayed, and hoped his strength and size would see him through. It would have to be a huge animal indeed, and very brave, to try and tackle Gerry, but she hadn't seen what was crashing through the woods, nor how many of them there had been, so she said another silent prayer and wished him well.

When she had her breath back, and some strength returned to her legs, Leanne set off on the final part of her journey, across the field that led to home. She decided to run straight across the field, rather than stick to the lane, as it would surely be quicker.

But Leane had forgotten about one of the side effects of leaving cows in fields without adequate supervision.

As she ran, she thought she saw frisbees lying in the grass. Giant frisbees, all the same dullish colour, though in the gloom it was hard to make out the colour of anything anymore. She wondered what they were doing in the field, for she couldn't imagine cows playing with frisbees, no matter how ridiculous the story in which they weren't even appearing.

And as she ran, she occasionally stepped on one of the frisbees, and was intrigued, or would have been if she hadn't still been in the grip of terror, to find that the frisbees had a kind of crunchy, crusty top. And when her feet went through the crusty, crunchy top, they entered a world of something soft and slippy.

And very, very smelly.

Leanne suddenly realized what she was stepping in, and at that moment, her feet went from under her and she felt herself flailing about, trying to get a grip on the not so very fresh air, and failing.

She windmilled around for a few moments, then found gravity inviting her back to earth, where she landed with a mixture of *Splat!* And *Thud!*

"Shplud!" she went.

"Ugh," she groaned, for though pigs are supposed to like rolling around in filth, they really only do it to keep cool on hot summer days. Leanne was fairly hot from running through the woods, but not so hot that she would have stopped to roll in the mud before she was safely home, and certainly not to roll in the stuff that comes gushing out of a cow's bottom and forms frisbee-like circles on the ground.

Like she said: Ugh.

Leanne stood up, covered in runny, smelly, cow dung, and feeling very sorry for herself.

"Momma will go mad when she sees this," she thought. "And she'll go even madder when she smells it."

At least, she told herself, she'll be so glad to see me safe and sound, she'll forget about the state I'm in, and she took a step towards the lights already glowing in her own front windows.

At that very same moment, a shadow appeared and blocked her way.

Leanne's brain registered the shadow and sent a message to her feet to stop moving. Then it instructed her eyes to check this shadow out, so it could figure out what it was and what evasive action, if any, was required to avoid it.

Leanne's eyes obeyed her brain and looked up, to find they were staring into another pair of eyes, as though someone had placed a big mirror in the middle of the field. And not an ordinary mirror, reflecting her own tiny, frightened eyes, but a mirror that turned those eyes into enormous, bloodshot orbs of concentrated badness.

Leanne's eyes reported back to her brain, and her brain swiftly worked out that she was staring into the eyes of a Wolf.

And not just any Wolf; this was the huge, snarling, heartless Wolf from all her worst nightmares, and Mommapig's worst stories.

The Wolf glared at Leanne as though she had done something unspeakable to him a long, long time ago, and he had been waiting for revenge ever since. Its tongue flopped out the side of its mouth as though it had a life of its own, dripping with slobber, and its eyes glittered in the light of the rising moon, reflecting all the compassion of an empty Universe.

Just in case Leanne wasn't feeling *completely* abandoned, she became aware that the wolf was not alone. Two slightly less gigantic companions emerged from the woods and began to circle and watch Leanne with the same pitiless gaze as their pack leader.

Leanne was beginning to think she was in a spot of bother.

Part of her brain wondered whether to try and engage them in conversation, try and divert their attention from hunger.

Onto what?

Things they had in common?

All she could think of in common with wolves was that they breathed, presumably, and occasionally slept?

And did they even speak Pig? She certainly wasn't fluent in Wolf, she knew that, and anyway, her mouth was so dry, she doubted she'd be able to open it, never mind speak, and - for Goodness Sakes! She was about to die, why was she having ridiculous conversations with herself?

She concentrated her thoughts on possible positive solutions.

Maybe the smell of cow dung clinging to her skin would put them off?

No. The ravenous way they watched her, saliva hanging from their jaws, told her they really weren't that bothered by a bit of manure. For all she knew, manure was a delicious gourmet sauce to a discriminating wolf.

She wondered if she could outrun them, and, though she knew it was impossible, had decided she had no other option but to try, Unfortunately, the wolves anticipated this move and positioned themselves to block off every avenue of escape.

She looked over their shoulders and could see the lights of home - so close, she could see the shape of someone moving past a window, someone who was probably wondering where she was, and who was powerless to help her. If Leanne had been thinking things couldn't possibly get any worse, now she had a broken heart to go with her despair.

And now it was raining!

Why should she care? The rain at least hid the tears falling from her own eyes, and she wouldn't be cold and wet for long. She would never be cold and wet again.

The wolves crept closer. Leanne could smell their rank, fetid breath, and she sank to the floor and closed her eyes. There was nothing she could do but accept what was about to happen.

Leanne could close her eyes, but she couldn't close her ears, and her ears could hear the panting and growling of wolves about to feast.

Her ears could hear paws, and claws, moving through the grass and the dung, and the rapid thumping of her own broken heart.

And her ears could hear the rumble of thunder, rapidly approaching, growing louder and louder, and they could hear the growling of the wolves mixing with whimpers and whines, and she opened her eyes and suddenly another figure appeared from the shadows, and the Wolves hunkered down, surprised, the fur standing up on their slinking shoulders.

The new arrival towered over them, and even as Leanne took to her trotters, the voice of Gerry Bull filled her ears, telling her, "Run, Leanne. Run. Fast as you can!"

Leanne ran, as fast as she could, while behind her rang the ever-diminishing grunts and howls of a titanic battle. Only once did she dare glance back, to see a terrible sight, a tableau she would see in her mind for many years to come; captured like a photograph, in dramatic, silvery moonlight,

Gerry stood tall, a Wolf lying still at his feet, a second held back by a mighty hoof to its throat, while a third stood angry on the young bull's back, claws digging deep, teeth and gums exposed beneath cruel upturned lips.

Leanne galloped away, out of the field, over the farm gate, across the yard, in through the door and collapsed on the floor, panting and heaving and sweating and safe.

At last.

She looked up, expecting to see worried faces, or at least one angry face, but all she saw was Mommapig mending socks with a needle and thread, and Grandmommapig sitting in her rocking chair, snoring.

After a few seconds of awkward silence, Mommapig looked at her without emotion, and calm as you like, said; "You'd better get yourself off to bed." And looking at the cow dung dripping off Leanne's face, added; "And you better get a good wash, first."

Then she turned away and carried on with her darning.

Leanne was too shocked to speak. She felt heartbroken. Forlorn and deserted, not to mention guilty, sad and ashamed.

She trudged off up the stairs, stopping to peer anxiously out through a window. More than anything, she wanted to go out and find Gerry, find out what had happened, but she knew there was no way she could help him, even if she weren't still overwhelmed with fear.

Besides, everything was dark and there was no sign of Gerry, or anyone or anything else.

She stood with her head in the sink, not sure if she was crying, because her tears were merging with the hot water and washing away down the drain, but she *felt* as though she were crying, felt as though she'd never been so sad in all her life, and that she could never be more sad, if she lived to be a hundred and twelve.

But she was wrong again, for when she went into her room, on the table by her bed, she found a glass of milk and a stack of biscuits.

Leanne threw herself on the bed, weeping and confused. She'd hurt Mommapig, she knew that, and Mommapig was hurt, and disappointed, and she hadn't said anything when Leanne landed through the door, dirty, dishevelled and frightened half to death, and that made Leanne feel ten times worse.

And *now*, she'd been and left her supper, showing she still loved her, no matter how upset or disappointed she was. It was almost too much to bear.

And what about when she learned what happened to the others?

And Gerry?

And what *had* happened to them?

This was definitely one of the worst days of Leanne's life, and she was relieved a couple of hours later when she finally cried herself to sleep.

Chapter 7

The next day, Leanne awoke, hoping she'd had the worst dream ever, but when she crept downstairs and saw Mommapig's face, she knew that was a hopeless dream itself.

Mommapig was bustling about as usual, getting breakfast ready, but she wouldn't look at Leanne or acknowledge her presence. Grandmommapig looked at her once, over her glasses, then went back to adjusting her dentures with grotesque sounds and unsettling movements of her tongue and jaw.

Leanne sat down without a word and waited to see what would happen next.

What happened next was, Mommapig brought over two bowls of Piggymush Breakfast Cereal and placed them on the table in front of them. Grandmommapig dived in snout first and was soon swilling food down her fat throat, but Leanne couldn't bear the thought of food, and she couldn't bear the thought of carrying on like this, with Mommapig not speaking to her or even looking at her.

Finally, with tears again beginning to rise behind her eyelids, she found the courage to speak herself.

"Momma," she said. "I'm really, really sorry."

Momma carried on with what she was doing. Grandmommapig, on the other hand, broke off from her disgusting feeding frenzy and looked at Leanne with food dripping off the hairs on her chinny-chin-chin.

"Ooh, you're sorry," she said sarcastically. "Oh boo hoo, well that makes everything all right, doesn't it? Poor Leanne. And what about your friends, eh? I bet they're sorry too. Oh yes, I bet they're *really* sorry, I bet they want to come and apologise, don't they? But, oh, wait a minute – they can't can they? Because they're DEAD!"

And she glared at Leanne until Leanne couldn't stop the tears from spilling out of her eye sockets and dripping into her bowl of mush.

"That's enough," Mommapig said quietly. "Leanne, go through to the other room. I'll bring you some milk in a minute."

Leanne stood up, shaking with emotion, and walked across the kitchen towards the other room. She wished she could go back in time and change everything.

She wished she'd never heard of Town, never mind persuaded everyone to go there.

She wished *she'd* been eaten by wolves, instead of Gerry.

She wished she'd never been born.

She heard a groaning, croaking, gasping sound, and realised it was herself, sobbing, and about to begin a session of uncontrollable weeping.

She pulled aside the curtain and stepped into the other room.

Immediately she sensed a presence.

She wasn't alone.

She tried to open her eyes, but her vision was blurry with tears. She blinked and rubbed her eyes, and thought she was going insane. She rubbed them again, not trusting the message she thought they had just sent to her brain, but when she looked again, she was astounded.

There in front of her were Lululamb, Carolyne Calf, Turkey Tess, Vinegar Joe - all the animals who had gone to town...and they were all alive!

Best of all – Gerry Bull was there, smiling at her from the back of the room.

Leanne felt dizzy, and happy, and sad.

And angry and confused, all at the same time.

She felt so many things, all at once, she nearly fell over. When she realized she wasn't insane, or imagining things, and that all her friends were really there, safe and sound, she turned round to find Mommapig standing behind her. Leanne hugged her with all her strength.

"I'm so sorry, Momma," she said. "I'll never do anything like that again."

"I know you won't," Mommapig told her. "It's okay."

"But I don't understand," Leanne said after a while. "What happened?"

"We all got the bus," Vinegar Joe called out. "That

was the plan." Vinnie noticed Gerry edging towards him with an angry frown, and decided not to say any more, but Leanne was searching the faces of all the animals, trying to figure out exactly what *had* happened.

"Momma?" she said.

"I'll tell you when everyone's gone," Mommapig promised. "Now let's all have some breakfast."

"Yes," squealed Grandmommapig from the table behind them. "More breakfast." Everyone turned and laughed when they saw her peering over the top of her bowl, Piggymush dripping from every wrinkle and crease in her ridiculous face.

"What?" she said. "What's up? What you all laughing at?"

Later, when everyone but Gerry had left, Leanne learned that when Gerry told everyone to meet at 9 o'clock, instead of going off to explore the town and risk being ambushed by Wolves, the friends secretly met up, round the corner, five minutes later. There they boarded a special bus which had brought them all back to the farm less than an hour after they had left. All except Gerry of course, who had to stay with Leanne for the plan to work.

"What plan?" Leanne asked. Gerry and Mommapig looked at each other, slightly ashamed.

"The plan to scare you into being good and staying safe," Mommapig said.

Leanne was still puzzled. "I'm still puzzled," she

said. Gerry spoke up.

"Mommapig knows you be goin' off on your own one day," he said, "and she was frightened as to what might happen. So, she asks me and our pals, if we wouldn't put on a little show for you, lets you see what *might* be happenin' if you goes wanderin' off on your own."

"So it was all made up?" Leanne said, not sure whether to be relieved or upset. She understood what they had tried to do, and it had certainly worked – she would definitely not be going to Town anytime soon, and definitely not on her own, and especially not at night; but couldn't they have done it another way?

"You really scared me," she said. "And I was so sad, thinking all my friends had been eaten by Wolves, and that you didn't love me anymore."

"I'm sorry," Mommapig said. "I just love you so much. I couldn't bear it if anything happened to you."

"I know," Leanne said, giving her another hug. "It was horrible. I'm never doing anything like that as long as I live. I'm going to have nightmares forever."

"You don't have to," Mommapig said. "You were never in danger; Gerry saw to that."

Leanne turned round and looked at Gerry.

"So all those noises I heard, thinking I was being followed, that was you?"

Gerry shuffled all four of his feet and looked slightly embarrassed.

"I suppose so," he said.

"And when I ran through the woods, thinking something was chasing me; that was you as well?"

"I'm afraid so," he confessed.

"And the Wolves? How did you get them to join in?"

"Wolves?" Mommapig looked up, puzzled.

"Wolves?" shouted Grandmommapig from the other room. "Where?"

Everyone ignored her. Leanne and Mommapig were watching Gerry trying to edge towards the door.

"Gerry?" Leanne said.

He looked up.

"What?"

"The Wolves?"

"Yes," Mommapig said. "The Wolves."

"What about 'em?"

"How did *they* get involved?" Mommapig was frowning. "They weren't part of the plan."

"No," Gerry said. "I know. They was just some friends of mine. I thoughts it would just add that final touch, you know?."

"Friends?" Momma said. "You have friends who are *Wolves*?"

"Nooo," Gerry gave a nervous laugh. "They was just *dressed* as Wolves. I wouldn't go messing with *real* Wolves. D'you thinks I'm mad?"

Mommapig looked at him uncertainly. She didn't think he was mad. She thought he was very brave, and kind, but still…

"Leave him alone, Momma," Leanne said. "You know he wouldn't let me be in danger. Come on," and she nudged Gerry towards the door. "Let's go and find the others so they can all have a good laugh at my expense."

Gerry gratefully moved towards the door, with a last bashful smile towards Mommapig, who still wore the ghost of a frown.

"Bye Mrs Mommapig," he said, and allowed Leanne to push him outside.

"Bye," Mommapig called after him. "Don't go far, Leanne."

"I won't," Leanne called back.

She followed Gerry into the yard, watching him closely.

"So," she said, catching him up. "They were friends of yours, were they?"

"Who?" Gerry pulled a puzzled face, as though he had no idea what she was talking about.

"The Wolves," Leanne said. "The ones in the

woods."

"Oh, those," he said. "Yes," he said. "I wonder where Vinnie is," he said.

He looked around and took a couple of steps towards the western field. Leanne studied him closely.

"Gerry," she said. "Was I ever in danger last night?"

Gerry turned reluctantly.

"Danger?"

"Danger."

"Well," he said. "You could've been run overs by a truck or something, I supposes."

"Not that kind of danger," Leanne said.

"Oh, right," he said. "Well, I supposes a tree could've blown down and landed on your head, like."

"Gerry!"

"What?"

"You know what," Leanne said. "Danger; like in Wolves, And teeth. Claws, blood. All that kind of stuff."

"Oh, ha ha," he laughed, unconvincingly. "Course not, you fool. Blood? Ha ha. As if…"

"Are you sure?" Leanne stared at him, watching his eyes, convinced he wasn't telling her everything. Gerry must have noticed, because he turned to face her then, wearing a serious expression.

"Look, Leanne," he said. "It's dangerous, that world out there. We all *knows* it, but we don't really *believes* it, or we don't *wants* to believe it; but it is. My old dad used to say; 'Gerry, you can't be learning from others' mistakes. I wishes you could, but you can't.' And it's true, it is. So me an' your mum, we decides to give you a fright, so's you can learns from your own mistakes, see? And I'm thinking it's worked, I am, and that's all there is to it."

Leanne looked at his big, kindly face, and she could see she was upsetting him, and that was the very last thing she wanted to do. She went up to him and gave him a big kiss on the cheek.

"Thank you Gerry," she said.

"I don't knows what for," he said, and if Bulls could blush, that's what he was doing.

"For looking out for me," she said. "Thanks."

"It were nothing," he said. "Why, if there *had* been Wolves, you wouldn't have seen me for dust, I promises you. I ain't no hero, an' you'd a probably been pork chops by now, I'm certain, I am."

He laughed and turned away, and Leanne laughed as well. But as he turned, the sun touched his back and reflected gently off his hide.

And Leanne thought she saw the sun's rays bouncing off something on top of Gerry's shoulders, as if there were something there. Something sticky, something like liquid, that was caked and drying up.

Something – just for example – like blood.

And as he walked away, she tried to get a better look, and it was hard for he was so much taller, but she swore she could see, raked along his broad, muscular shoulders, marks and scratches, deep and red, that may have been made by – just for example – the claws of a Wolf.

Try as she might, she couldn't get a proper look, and from that day to this, Gerry hasn't said a thing about what happened the night they went to Town, and Leanne has never asked him.

But, deep in her heart, she knew.

The End